Ridiculous Riddles for Kids

I0803926

ISBN 978-1-64124-143-4

To learn more about the other great books from Fox Chapel Publishing, or to find a retailer near you, call toll-free
800-457-9112 or visit us at *www.FoxChapelPublishing.com*.

We are always looking for talented authors. To submit an idea, please send a brief inquiry to acquisitions@foxchapelpublishing.com.

Fox Chapel Publishing makes every effort to use environmentally friendly paper for printing.

Printed in China
First printing

Kid Scoop ON THE GO

Ridiculous Riddles for Kids

Mysterious Puzzles, Secret Codes, and Brain Teasers to Unravel and Solve!

Happy Fox BOOKS

Vicki Whiting

Illustrated by

Jeff Schinkel

"All is a riddle, and the key to a riddle is another riddle."

– RALPH WALDO EMERSON

Ridiculous Riddles for Kids

What is a Riddle?

Simply put, riddles are something challenging to understand. Sometimes they are a question with a surprising answer. Riddles make you think. And when you find the answer to the riddle, you might just feel a little smarter, or start laughing!

PRESENTING THE WORLD'S OLDEST RIDDLE

Riddles have been entertaining and challenging people for at least 4,000 years! The oldest riddle that was written down is from Ancient Sumeria, which was located where Iraq is today. It was written about 1900 B.C.

Ancient Sumeria is also the civilization with the oldest surviving writing system!

Here's the world's oldest riddle. Can you figure out the answer? Think it over, make a guess, then circle every other letter to see if you guessed correctly.

"There is a house. One enters it blind and comes out seeing. What is it?"

ACSBCNHROSOT
LVHCOSUNSWER

_ _ _ _ _ _ _ _ _ _ _ _   _

The Riddle of the Sphinx*

Throughout history, heroes in tales have had to solve riddles to save others or travel to certain places. In one Greek myth, the hero must solve the riddle posed by the Sphinx guarding the city of Thebes.

The Sphinx was a mythical creature with the body of a lion, the head of a human, and the wings of an eagle. And as the guardian of Thebes, it **ate** the people who could not answer this tricky riddle!

Can YOU answer it?

"What animal walks on four legs in the morning, two legs at noon, and three legs at night?"

Think about it. Then, circle every other letter to reveal the answer.

A B H C U Y M J A S N
V B W E L I K N C G B

A H _ _ _ _ _
_ _ _ _ _

How can this be? Hold this page up to a mirror for the explanation.

When we are babies we crawl on all fours, as an adult we walk on two legs, in old age we need a third leg (a walking stick).

*No, the *OTHER* Sphinx!

Sphinxes appear in the art and legends of both ancient Greece and ancient Egypt. Ancient Egyptians made many large statues of sphinxes. The largest and most famous Egyptian sphinx was carved near the pyramids of Giza in about 2500 B.C.

King Odin's Riddles

Odin is the Norse god of wisdom, poetry, death, and magic. Odin is also the king of the mythological land of Asgard. (You may remember from comic books or movies that his sons were Thor and Loki.)

In ancient Viking myths, riddles are used to test intelligence and wisdom. One Norse myth about three mythological characters, King Odin, King Heidrek, and Gestumblindi, is a tale full of riddles.

To save Gestumblindi's life, Odin asks King Heidrek 35 riddles. To do this, Odin poses as Gestumblindi. King Heidrek gets them all correct.

But he also figures out that it is Odin and not Gestumblindi asking the riddles. King Heidrek becomes furious and tries to kill Odin. Odin magically turns into a hawk and flies away!

Use King Odin's Secret Code to solve the riddles.

Odin's Riddle #1

Thirty white horses on a red hill
First they champ,
Then they stamp,
Then they stand still.
King Heidrek,
Guess my riddle.

Odin's Riddle #2

Who is that great one
Who grasps the earth,
Swallowing wood and water.
Bad weather he dreads,
Wind, but no man,
And picks a fight with the sun.
King Heidrek,
Guess my riddle.

Three Ancient Riddles

These three riddles have been around longer than anyone can remember. Unscramble the words to reveal the answers.

1. What is so fragile that just saying its name breaks it?

NLICEES

_ _ _ _ _ _ _

2. What goes through cities and fields but never moves?

SDORA

_ _ _ _ _

3. What can fill a room but takes no space at all?

GHITL

_ _ _ _ _

The Riddle of the Two-Headed Dragon

You are traveling in a mythical land. In your travels you come to a fork in the road that is guarded by a huge two-headed dragon.

The dragon explains to you that one of its heads always speaks the **truth**, while the other always speaks **lies**.

One of the roads from the fork leads to terrible danger, while the other leads to safety.

The dragon tells you that you are allowed to ask just one question to one of the dragon's heads in order to determine which path leads to safety and which one leads to danger.

The problem is, you don't know which head speaks truth and which one speaks lies.

What one question can you ask of either head to determine which road leads to safety?

Write the letter of the alphabet that comes before the letter under each line to reveal the answer.

X I J D I   S P B E

X P V M E   Z P V S

P U I F S   I F B E

U F M M   N F   U P

D I P P T F ?

Hold this page up to a mirror to see why that question will save you:

No matter which head you ask the question, you'll get the same answer directing you to take one of the roads. Whichever road you receive as the answer, you then take the opposite road to safety.

The Riddle of the Fishermen

In this ancient riddle, two fishermen posed a riddle to the Greek poet Homer. Poor Homer could never solve it. Can you? (It might make you a little itchy!)

What we caught,
we threw away;
what we didn't catch, we kept.
What did we keep?

Write the letter of the alphabet that comes before the letter under each line to reveal the answer.

___ ___ ___   ___ ___ ___ ___
U I F   M J D F

___ ___   ___ ___ ___ ___ ___
P O   U I F J S

___ ___ ___ ___ ___ ___!
C P E J F T

The Road to St. Ives

This rhyming riddle has been a favorite for hundreds of years. Can you solve it?

As I was going to St. Ives,
I met a man with seven wives,
Every wife had seven sacks,
Every sack had seven cats,
Every cat had seven kits.*
Kits, cats, sacks, and wives,
How many were going to St. Ives?

*Kits is short for kittens.

Did you figure out the answer? Number the sentences in the correct order to see if you are right!

were traveling in

to St. Ives. The others

the only one going

The person that was

the opposite direction.

telling this story was

Pilgrim Riddles

The Plimoth Patuxet Museums collected riddles from the 1600s. Draw a line from each riddle to the picture it describes.

EXAMPLE:
I went to the woods and I caught it,
I sat me down and I sought it,
But since I could not find it,
Home with me I brought it?
What is it?

ANSWER: A splinter!

Who is he that runneth through the hedge, his house on his back?

What is higher than a house and yet seems smaller than a mouse?

What is ten men's length and ten men's strength and yet ten men can never make it stand on its end?

What is full all day and empty at night?

Tricky Twitchett

This is a very old riddle poem. *Hint: Old Mother Twitchett is not a person.* After you guess the answer, use the code to reveal the solution.

Old Mother Twitchett had one eye,
And a long tail which she let fly.
And every time she went over a gap,
She left a bit of her tail in a trap.
What is Old Mother Twitchett?

26 = A	13 = N
25 = B	12 = O
24 = C	11 = P
23 = D	10 = Q
22 = E	9 = R
21 = F	8 = S
20 = G	7 = T
19 = H	6 = U
18 = I	5 = V
17 = J	4 = W
16 = K	3 = X
15 = L	2 = Y
14 = M	1 = Z

___ ___ ___
12 15 23

___ ___ ___ ___ ___ ___
14 12 7 19 22 9

___ ___ ___ ___ ___ ___ ___ ___ ___
7 4 18 7 24 19 22 7 7

___ ___ ___
18 8 26

___ ___ ___ ___ ___ ___
13 22 22 23 15 22

___ ___ ___
26 13 23

___ ___ ___ ___ ___ ___
7 19 9 22 26 23

A Cool Riddle

To discover the answer to this riddle, color the even-numbered squares BLUE and the odd-numbered squares YELLOW.

A precious stone,
As clear as diamond.
Seek it out when
The sun's near the horizon.
Though you can walk on water
With its power,
Try to keep it,
And it'll vanish in an hour.

9	8	7	6	4	6	1	8	2	6	5
5	2	5	8	3	7	5	6	5	1	7
1	4	3	2	1	5	7	4	1	9	5
3	6	9	4	5	7	5	2	8	2	5
7	8	9	2	9	5	9	2	7	9	3
5	4	1	4	5	3	7	4	9	7	3
9	6	7	8	1	9	3	6	5	1	9
7	2	5	6	2	4	5	8	4	2	5

Little Nanny Etticoat

Can you guess the answer to this rhyming riddle?
Connect the dots to reveal the answer.

Little Nanny Etticoat,
In a white petticoat,
And a red nose.
The longer she stands,
The shorter she grows.
What is she?

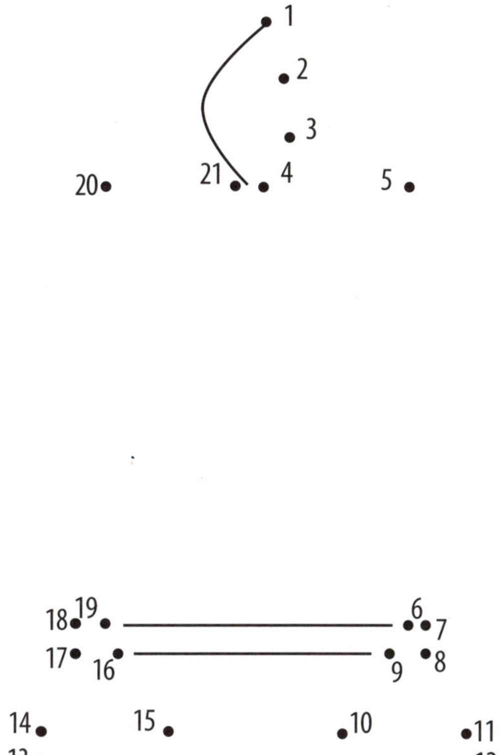

CLASSIC RIDDLES

Time for T

Think about this one for a bit before using the code to solve the riddle.

Thomas T. Tattamus
took two twines,
to tie two twigs
to two tall trees,
to frighten the terrible
Tyler T. Tattamus!

Tell me how many T's
there are in THAT!

26 = A	13 = N
25 = B	12 = O
24 = C	11 = P
23 = D	10 = Q
22 = E	9 = R
21 = F	8 = S
20 = G	7 = T
19 = H	6 = U
18 = I	5 = V
17 = J	4 = W
16 = K	3 = X
15 = L	2 = Y
14 = M	1 = Z

__ __ __ __ __
7 19 22 9 22

__ __ __
26 9 22

__ __ __ __ ' __
7 4 12 7 ' 8

__ __ __ __ __
18 13 7 19 22

__ __ __ __
4 12 9 23

__ __ __ __
7 19 26 7

Scrambled Mystery

**In marble walls as white as milk,
Lined with a skin as soft as silk,
Within a fountain crystal clear,
A golden apple doth appear.
No doors there are to this stronghold,
Yet thieves break in and steal the gold.
What am I?**

To reveal the answer, cross out the words that rhyme with MOOSE, LAMP, CORE, SPIN, and SEAT.

**TIN GOOSE CAMP
DOOR CLAMP STAMP
PIN AN STORE FIN
TRUCE SPRUCE WIN
FLOOR EGG DAMP
EAT CHORE FLEET**

Let's Be Clear

This old riddle will keep you guessing. To discover the answer, write down the letters along the correct path through the maze.

I can be all the colors of the rainbow or no color at all. Sometimes I'm empty, and sometimes I'm full.

Cast a Spell

Circle every third letter to reveal the answer to this old riddle.

Which word in the dictionary is always spelled incorrectly?

G B I W R N

D Q C K L O

P M R F C R

S V E H T C R

R T U B L I G Y

_ _ _ _ _ _ _ _ _ _ _

What Is It?

To solve this classic riddle, write the answers to the questions in the boxes on the next page. The letters that appear in the pink boxes will spell the answer.

**You use me from head to toe.
The more I work, the smaller I grow.
What am I?**

1. The sandy place where the ocean meets the shore.
2. An activity you do for fun, such as making pottery, fishing, oil painting, etc.
3. A loud sound used to wake you up or alert you of danger.
4. Another word for mistake, often seen when working on a computer.
5. A kitchen tool used for serving ice cream.
6. Halfway to one hundred.
7. Another name for macaroni, spaghetti, lasagne, and other noodles.
8. The opposite of tall.
9. The organ you are using to think of answers to all these questions.
10. The opposite of sad.

1.					
2.	H				
3.				R	
4.					
5.					
6.					
7.					A
8.					
9.					
10.					

Say It With Pictures

A **rebus** is a word or a phrase spelled out in pictures and letters. One of the most famous is

___ A ___ ___ ___

___ ___ ___ ___ ___ ___ ___ Y

___ ___ ___ ___ ___

- AIRS
-H
-KE
-AT

___ ___ ___ ___ ___

___ ___

___ ___

M +
is
Y +
- DO

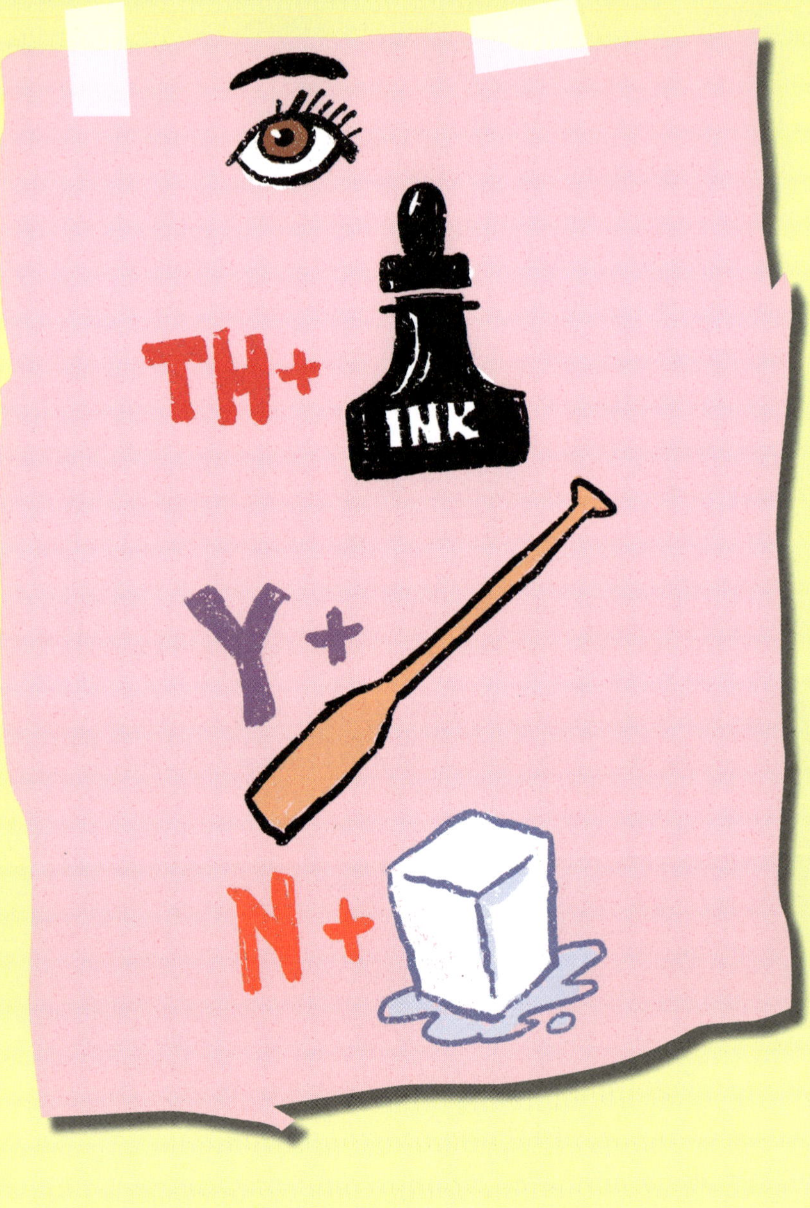
TH+
INK
Y+
N+

___ ___ ___ ___ ___ ___

___ ___ ___ ' ___ ___

___ ___ ___ ___

+n't
2
L+8

___ ___ ___ ' ___

___ ___ ___ ___ ___

___ ___ ___ ___

___ ___ ___   ___ ___ ___ ___

W +
+ T
2

___ ___ ___ ___ ___ ___'___

___ ___ ___

___ ___ ___?

-E
B+
-V

___ ___ ___ ___ ___ ___

___ ___ ___ ___ ___

___ ___ ___ ___

Odd Word Out

In each group of words, circle the word that does not belong.

turpentine carpentry
serpent competition
suspense penguin
opening expensive

Why did you choose this word?

____

sun hare
flower bee
star bear
rose sea

Why did you choose this word?

____

LINCOLN ROOSEVELT JEFFERSON WILSON FRANKLIN JOHNSON CLEVELAND TRUMAN TAFT REAGAN McKINLEY

Why did you choose this word?

____

pants moose news tuna sheep mice elk scissors furniture binoculars

Why did you choose this word?

____

Time Crunch

Each of these clocks shows a time between 12:00 noon and 7:00 p.m.
Can you number them in order in under two minutes? GO!

License 2 Laugh

Can you decide which license plate belongs to which driver?

___ an electric car owner

___ an airline pilot

___ a music teacher

___ a farmer

___ a cheerleader

___ a doctor

___ a golfer

___ a movie director

___ a zookeeper

___ a comedian

Mystery Spot

Use the pictures to create words. Then write each numbered letter where it belongs to reveal the joke's punch line.

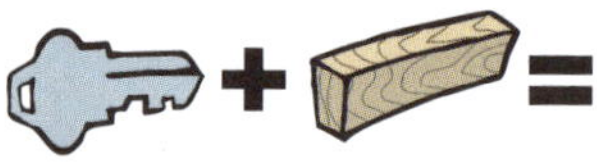 ___ ___(2) ___ ___ ___ ___ ___ ___

 ___ ___(9) ___ ___ ___   ___ ___ ___ ___ ___ ___(10)

 ___(8) ___(4) ___ ___ ___ ___ ___ ___ ___

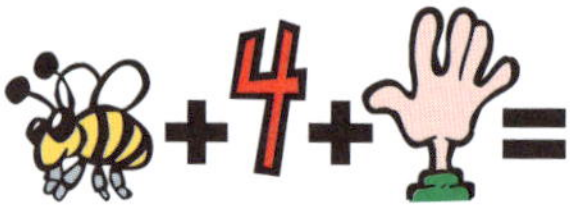 ___ ___ ___ ___ ___ ___ ___(3) ___ ___(6) ___

 ___(12) ___(1) ___ ___ ___ ___(7) ___ ___

 ___(5) ___ ___ ___ ___ ___ ___(11) ___ ___ ___

Why did the clown stuff a $20 bill in the gumball machine?

___ ___   ___ ___ ___   ___ ___
1 2   3 4 5   6 7

___ ___ ___ ___ ___
8 9 10 11 12

Out-of-the-Box Thinking

Only one of the shapes can be folded into a box with four sides, a top and a bottom, and no extra flaps. Think it over carefully, then draw the shape you think will make a complete box on another sheet of paper. Cut it out and fold it to see if you guessed correctly!

A

C

B

D

E

F

Picnic Puzzler

Use the pictures to help you fill in the squares on this picnic blanket.

Idioms are Funny Phrases

An idiom is a common phrase that means something different from what the actual words say. Look at the common idioms below. Then match each idiom with its meaning by writing the correct number next to that idiom's definition.

1. That will happen when pigs fly.

2. Get your ducks in a row.

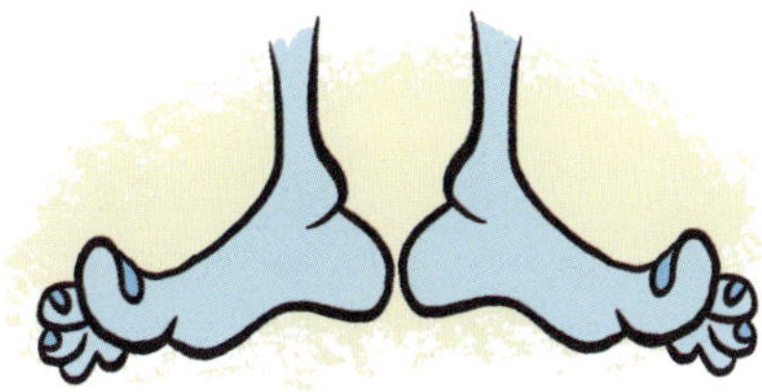

3. He's getting cold feet.

4. Don't count your chickens before they're hatched.

5. She's been feeling under the weather.

6. I felt like a fish out of water.

____ Nervous or reluctant
____ Don't be too sure
____ In an unfamiliar place
____ Something that's impossible
____ Be organized
____ Sick or unwell

I See What You Mean

Each word-picture puzzle has a meaning. Work with a parent to figure them out.

1

2

3

4

5

THORNROSETHORN

6

Ghostly Gallery

When they were alive, each member of the Bones family had a favorite hobby. Can you match each portrait with a hobby?

The Claw!

Strong claws and a hard outer shell make the American lobster one tough crustacean. It is aggressive and territorial. Whenever it can, it steals bait from traps and food from the homes of other lobsters. This has earned lobsters a nickname.

Use the code to crack the mystery of the lobster's nickname.

Combinations

Flytrap is a **compound word**, made by combining two smaller words: ***fly*** and ***trap***. Look at the pictures below. Draw a line between two pictures to make a compound word. Write the word, then write each numbered letter where it belongs to reveal the joke's punch line.

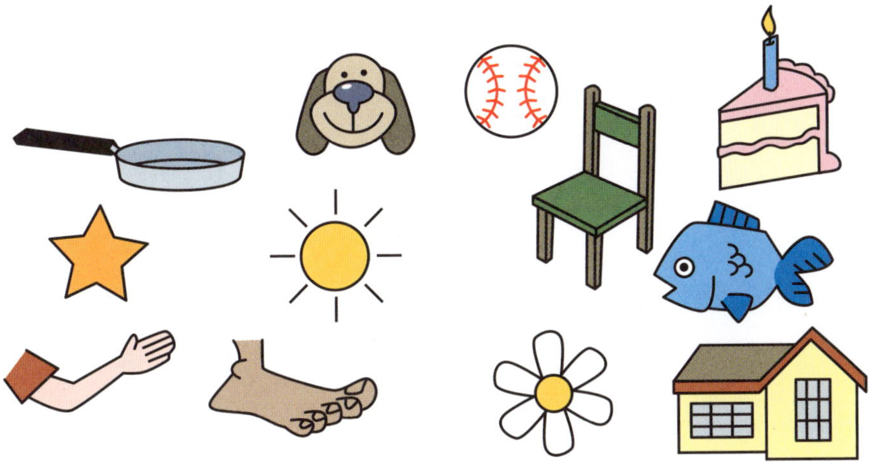

_ _ _ _ H (1) _ _

_ _ _ F (5) _ (6) _ _

(2) _ _ _ F _ _ _ _

_ (7) G _ _ _ _ (8)

(3) _ _ C _ (4) _

_ _ (9) _ B _ _ _

What do you get when you cross a porcupine with a snail?

_ _ _ _ _ _ _ _ _

1 2 5 7 6 3 9 4 8

What a Pane!

Circle every other letter to reveal the answer to this riddle.

Why did the teacher write on the window?

S W O J T V H X E
I L F E D S G S M
O U N P W K A H S
H V T E O R I Y D
C B L T E Y A M R

S __ __ __ __

__ __ __ __ __ __

__ __ __ __ __ __ __

__ __ __ __ __

By the Book

On each line, write the letter that comes before the letter under that line to discover the punch line to this riddle.

C F D B V T F

D M P D L T

U P D L U P P

N V D I

The Farmer's Crossing

This tricky riddle has been around for hundreds of years. Can you solve it?

A farmer is returning home from the market. He has a chicken, a bag of grain, and a fox with him. But when he reaches a river, the small raft he must use only has room for the farmer and one other item. He'll need to make more than one trip to get them all across the river.

If the farmer leaves the fox with the chicken, the fox will eat the chicken. But if he leaves the chicken with the bag of grain, the chicken will eat the grain.

How can the farmer get them all to the other side of the river?

Number the panels in order to explain how the farmer can get the chicken, grain and fox across the river.

What did the birthday card say to the stamp?

"Stick with me.
We're going places!"

What does every birthday end with?

The
letter Y.

What goes up but never comes down?

Your age.

Why do people always light candles on top of birthday cakes?

They're too hard to light beneath birthday cakes.

What is a carrot's favorite soda?

Root beer.

What do you call a big plate of fake spaghetti?

An impasta.

Why do people seldom order plain popcorn?

Because there are butter ones out there.

Why will a chef never eat his apron?

It goes against his stomach.

How did the monster feel after he ate an apartment building?

A little homesick.

How do monsters like their eggs cooked for breakfast?

Terror-fried.

Why did the bats run out of birthday party favors?

Because they forgot to count Dracula.

What happens if a vampire forgets to brush his teeth?

He gets bat breath.

Why did the bank robber take a bath after every robbery?

To make a clean getaway.

Who will always try to steal the soap from your bathtub?

Robber duckies.

Which dogs love taking bubble baths?

Shampoodles.

What did the giant say after he took a bath in the harbor?

"Thank you for your soap port!"

What do gorillas and chimpanzees learn in school?

Their Ape B C's.

What's the best way to make sure you always get straight A's?

Use a ruler.

What do you get by throwing a lot of books into the sea?

A title wave.

Why did the toilet paper roll down the hill?

To get to the bottom.

Three bears were under one tiny umbrella. How did they stay dry?

Circle every other letter.

I B T E W N A W S V N P O G
T Y R B A N I L N R I A N F G

IT W___ ___ ________

What kind of bow can never be tied?

Use the code to reveal the answer!

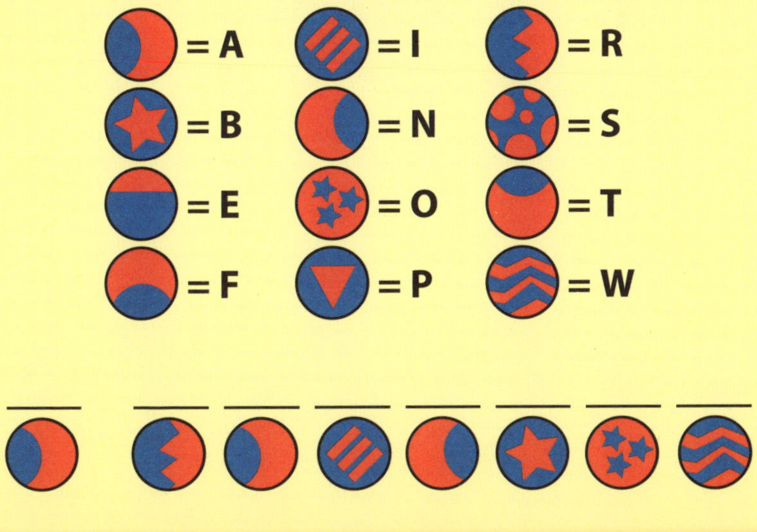

It's All Relative

In an art gallery, a man is looking at a portrait. His friend asks, "Who is the man in that painting?"

The man replies, "Brothers and sisters, I have none. But that man's father is my father's son."

Who is in the portrait? Think it over, then write your answer under the painting.

December Riddle

Circle every third letter to reveal the answer to this riddle.

"I belong in the month of December, but not in any other month. I am not a holiday, and I have nothing to do with the temperature. What am I?"

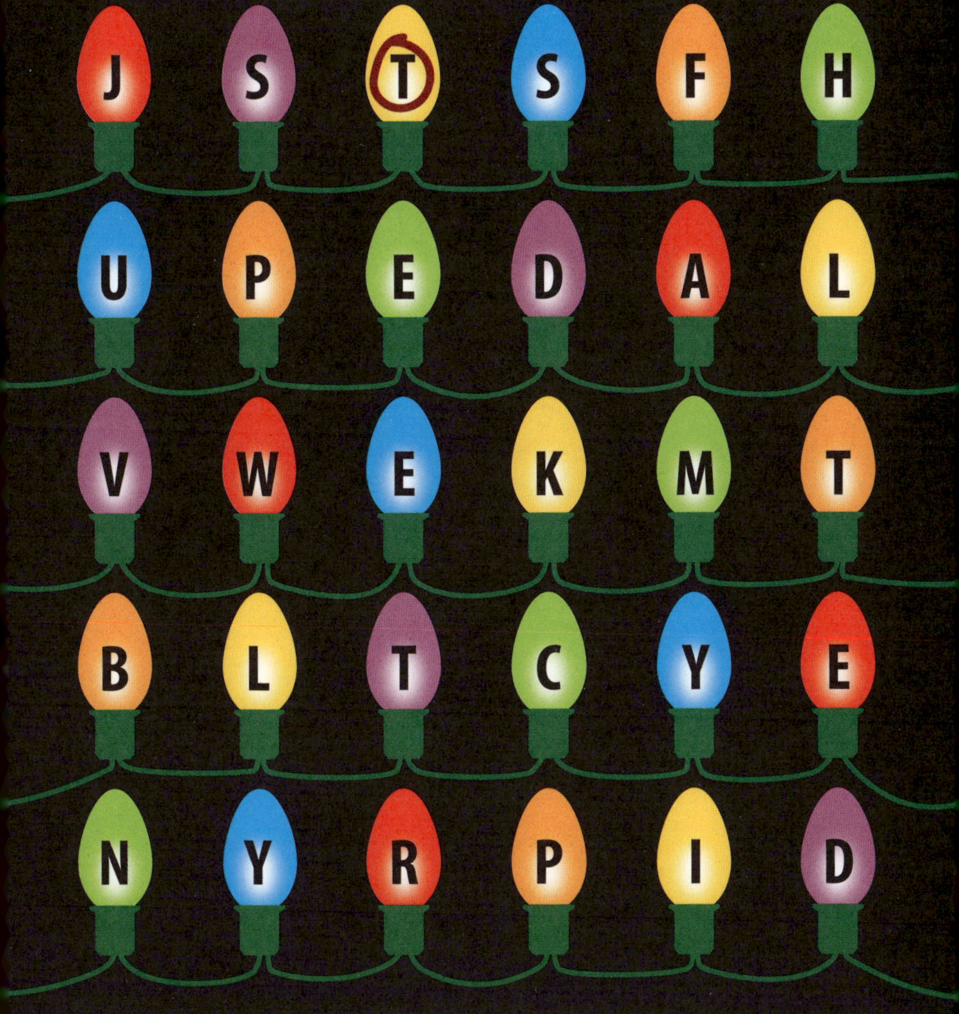

T___ ___ ___   ___ ___ ___ ___ ___ ___   ___

Out of Reach

Unscramble the letters along the correct path of the maze to reveal the answer.

Purple, yellow, red, and green,
The king cannot reach it,
Nor can the queen.
Nor can the wizard,
Whose power's so great.
Now answer this riddle
While I count eight.

By the Numbers

Think about this one for a bit before using the code to solve the riddle.

How is seven different from the other numbers from one to ten?

26 = A	13 = N
25 = B	12 = O
24 = C	11 = P
23 = D	10 = Q
22 = E	9 = R
21 = F	8 = S
20 = G	7 = T
19 = H	6 = U
18 = I	5 = V
17 = J	4 = W
16 = K	3 = X
15 = L	2 = Y
14 = M	1 = Z

26 15 15   7 19 22

13 6 14 25 22 9 8

19 26 5 22   12 13 22

8 2 15 15 26 25 15 22

22 3 24 22 11 7

8 22 5 22 13

On the Right Track

An electric train is travelling **north** at 50 miles per hour. The wind is blowing **east** at 70 miles per hour. Which direction will the smoke travel?

Circle every other letter to reveal the answer.

AEBLGEMCLT
NRJIVCWTQR
BALIYNASTD
FOZNLOPTX
PCRTOJD
CUACFEN
SBMWOVKHE

_ _ _ _ _ _ _ _

_ _ _ _ _ _

_ _   _ _ _

_ _ _ _ _ _ _

_ _ _ _ _

Off the Wall

Write the letters on the bricks in order to reveal the answer to this riddle.

Two ancient inventions, one that allows us to see through walls and the other that allows us to walk through walls, are still in use today. What are they?

15 S 5 O 12 O 6 W

14 R 10 D 8 A

13 O 3 N 2 I 1 W

4 D 7 S 11 D 9 N

___ ___ ___ ___ ___ ___ ___
1 2 3 4 5 6 7

___ ___ ___
8 9 10

___ ___ ___ ___ ___
11 12 13 14 15

Head in the Clouds

Read this riddle to a friend or family member. Can they guess the answer in less than 60 seconds? Unscramble the letters to reveal the answer.

I love to move around,
But usually not on the ground.
I'm quite strung out when way up high.
I like to sail, but I need to stay dry.
I need air, but not to breathe.
A helpful hand is all I need.
What am I?

A T I A K I E M

_ _ _ _

_ _ _ _

By the Numbers

One of these words does not belong. Can you figure out which one it is and why? Hold this page up to a mirror for the answer.

BRAWL
CARROT
CHANGE
CLOVER
PROPER SACRED
STONE SWING
SEVENTY
TRAVEL

All of the words except carrot will become another word when you remove the first and last letter.

Colorful Coat

What coats have no sleeves, no buttons, no fronts, no backs, and are always put on wet?

To reveal the answer, cross out the words that rhyme with CAT, BUBBLE, FIT, CAR, PAN, and TREE.

STAR HAT MITT FAR
COATS FREE DOUBLE
SAT TROUBLE PLAN
HIT OF ME JAR
SPLIT FLAT MAN
VAN PAINT TAR SEA
KEY RUBBLE MAT

Chomp! Chomp!

There's something fishy about this riddle. Circle every other letter to reveal the answer.

How many fish can a hungry piranha eat on an empty stomach?

S O E N V E G B N E A C G A H U J S W E
N A B F S T J E Z R P T G H I A L T M I C T F
S B S N T R O Y M F A M C L H T I
R S Q N X O Y L W O P N J G H E
C R V E K M L P I T C Y

O _ _, _ _ _ _ _ _ _

_ _ _ _ _ _ _ _ _ _ _ _ _ _ _ _

_ _ _ _ _ _ _ _ _ _ _ _ _ _ _

_ _ _ _ _ _ _ _ _ _ _ _ _ _ _

What do you call two octopuses that look exactly alike?

ANSWER: Tentacle twins!

What do you get when you cross an elephant with a computer?

ANSWER: A computer with extra memory.

ANSWERS

Page 6
A schoolhouse

Page 7
A human being

Page 8
Odin's Riddle #1
Teeth

Odin's Riddle #2
Fog

Page 9
1. Silence
2. Roads
3. Light

Page 10
Which road would your other head tell me to choose?

Page 13
The lice on their bodies!

Page 14
5 were traveling in
4 to St. Ives. The others
3 the only one going
1 The person that was
6 the opposite direction.
2 telling this story was

Page 16

Page 17
Old Mother Twitchett is a needle and thread

Page 18
Ice

Page 19
Candle

Page 20
There are two T's in the word THAT

Page 21
An egg

Page 22

Page 23
Incorrectly

Page 25
A bar of soap

1. Beach
2. Hobby
3. Alarm
4. Error
5. Scoop
6. Fifty
7. Pasta
8. Short
9. Brain
10. Happy

Page 27
Happy birthday to you

Page 28
Stand by me

Page 29
My house is your house

Page 30
I think you're nice

Page 31
Don't leave home too late

Page 32
Why can't I go too?

Page 33
Father knows best

Page 34
Yellow group: competition
All the other words contain the word "pen."

Blue group: star
All the other words are homophones.

Page 35
Green group: Franklin
All the others were presidents.

Purple group: mice
All the other words are the same in both singular and plural forms.

Page 36

Page 37
C an electric car owner
J an airline pilot
H a music teacher
I a farmer
B a cheerleader
F a doctor
G a golfer
E a movie director
A a zookeeper
D a comedian

Page 38

KEYBOARD (E 2)
BELLY BUTTON (E 9, N 10)
CARPENTRY (C 8, A 4)
BEFOREHAND (H 3, N 6)
SHOEHORN (S 12, H 1, O 7)
DELIGHTFUL (D 5, T 11)

Why did the clown stuff a $20 bill in the gumball machine?
He had no cents

Page 39
C

Page 40

Page 41
3 Nervous or reluctant
4 Don't be too sure
6 In an unfamiliar place
1 Something that's impossible
2 Be organized
5 Sick or unwell

Page 42
1. Jack-in-the-box
2. Ants in the pants
3. Brain drain
4. Burning the midnight oil
5. A rose between two thorns
6. Uphill, downhill

Page 43

Page 44
Gangster of the sea

Page 45
ARMCHAIR (1) SUNFLOWER (5, 6)
STARFISH (2) DOGHOUSE (7, 8)
PANCAKE (3, 4) FOOTBALL (9)

What do you get when you cross a porcupine with a snail?
A slowpoke

Page 46
So the lesson was very clear

Page 47
Because clocks tock too much

Page 49

Page 60
It was not raining

Page 61
A rainbow

Page 62
The viewer's son

Page 63
The letter D

Page 64
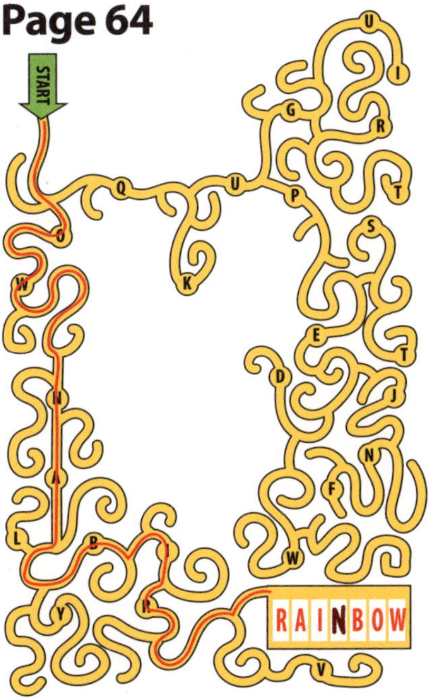

Page 65
All the numbers have one syllable except seven

Page 66
Electric trains do not produce smoke

Page 67
Windows and doors

Page 68
I am a kite

Page 70
Coats of paint

Page 71
One, because after that its stomach is no longer empty

Who made this book?

Ridiculous Riddles for Kids was made by the people who bring the weekly *Kid Scoop* page to hundreds of newspapers!

***Kid Scoop* believes learning is fun!** Our educational activity pages teach and entertain. Teachers use the page in schools to promote standards-based learning. Parents use the *Kid Scoop* materials to foster academic success, a joy of learning, and family discussions. Our fun puzzles and activities draw children into the page. This stimulates a child's interest and they then read the text.

When Fox Chapel discovered *Kid Scoop*, they knew that there were lots of kids looking for books just like this one!

Vicki Whiting – Author

Vicki was a third-grade teacher for many years. Now she loves teaching kids through the weekly entertaining and educational *Kid Scoop* page. People often ask where she gets her ideas for each week's page. Vicki says, "I listen to the questions kids ask. We answer those questions with every *Kid Scoop* page!"

Jeff Schinkel – Illustrator

Jeff has loved to draw his whole life! As a kid, sometimes he was drawing when he should have been listening to the teacher in class. He earned a BFA in Illustration at the Academy of Art University in San Francisco, where drawing in class is highly encouraged. Jeff is now a member of the National Cartoonists Society.

Vivien Whittington – Operations Manager

Vivien is a voracious reader! She always wanted to work in publishing and after getting a degree in Fine Art, worked in publishing houses in London, England, starting as a researcher and leaving as a senior editor. Vivien coordinates the *Kid Scoop* team to complete around 50 different page deadlines a month—like an air traffic controller!

Eli Smith – Graphic Designer, Webmaster

Eli grew up in Cazadero, California, population 420, near the Russian River. He received a graphics degree from Santa Rosa Junior College and became interested in visual arts through his father, who is a painter. Eli is an accomplished photographer and spends weekends hiking and photographing the hills and beaches of Sonoma County.

Collect them all!

1. Super Silly Jokes for Kids
   978-1-64124-067-3
2. Puzzling Pictures for Eagle-Eyed Kids
   978-1-64124-066-6
3. Super Funny Knock Knock Jokes for Kids
   978-1-64124-142-7
4. Super Fun Road Trip Activities for Kids
   978-1-64124-240-0
5. Mind-Boggling Animal Puzzles for Kids
   978-1-64124-241-7
6. Awesome Funny Fill-Ins for Kids
   978-1-64124-238-7
7. Brain-Bending Animal Puzzles for Kids
   978-1-64124-242-4
8. Super Funny Fill-Ins for Kids
   978-1-64124-239-4
9. Awesome Bird Puzzles for Kids
   978-1-64124-245-5
10. Terrific Travel Fun for Kids
    978-1-64124-243-1
11. Sensational Snow Day Puzzle for Kids
    978-1-64124-244-8